Flowers with Wings

Photographs by
Deborah Carney and Vinny O'Hare

A Collection of Beautiful Butterfly Photos

May the wings of the butterfly kiss the sun.
And find your shoulder to light on.
To bring you luck, happiness and riches.
Today, tomorrow and beyond.
~ An Irish Blessing ~

To Get **Flowers With Wings**, *Volume 2,* click the link below:
http://loxly.com/go/butterfly2

For Funky Butterfly Art:
http://loxly.com/go/funkybutterfly

See more Butterfly photos plus butterfly art and more books at:
http://CoolButterflies.com

One of the smallest butterflies:
Asian Atala Hairstreak

The toad beneath the harrow knows
Exactly where each tooth-point goes;
The butterfly upon the road
Preaches contentment to that toad.
~ Rudyard Kipling ~

Black and White Longwing Butterfly

Not for a moment, beautiful aged Walt
Whitman, have I failed to see your beard full of
butterflies.
~ *Federico Garcia Lorca* ~

Banded Purplewing Butterfly

I only ask to be free.
The butterflies are free.
~ Charles Dickens ~

Blue Cracker Butterfly

Happiness is a butterfly,
which when pursued,
is always just beyond your grasp,
but which, if you will sit down quietly,
may alight upon you.
~ Nathaniel Hawthorne, 1804-1864 ~

Blue Clipper Butterfly

The Butterfly's assumption-gown,
In chrysoprase apartments hung,
This afternoon put on.
How condescending to descend,
And be of buttercups the friend
In a New England town!
~ *Emily Dickinson* ~

Blue Glassy Tiger Butterfly

The air is like a butterfly
With frail blue wings
The happy earth looks at the sky
And sings.
~ Joyce Kilmer ~

Blue Morpho Butterfly

The butterfly is a flying flower,
The flower a tethered butterfly.
~ Ecouchard Le Brun ~

Brown Clipper Butterfly

I dreamed I was a butterfly,
flitting around in the sky; then I awoke.
Now I wonder:
Am I a man who dreamt of being a butterfly,
or am I a butterfly dreaming that I am a man?
~ Zhuangzi, Chinese Philosopher 369 - 286 BC~

Common Mormon Butterfly

Two butterflies went out at noon
And waltzed above a stream,
Then stepped straight through the firmament
And rested on a beam;

(continued...)

**Close-up of the wing of a Cream Owl
Butterfly**

And then together bore away
Upon a shining sea,
Though never yet, in any port,
Their coming mentioned be.

(continued...)

Doris Longwing Butterfly

If spoken by the distant bird,
If met in ether sea
By frigate or by merchantman,
Report was not to me.

~ Emily Dickinson ~

Great Eggfly Butterfly

Just living is not enough said the butterfly,
one must have sunshine, freedom and a little
flower.
~ Hans Christian Anderson ~

Green Banded Peacock Butterfly

Watching a butterfly for 5 minutes will lower
your blood pressure by 10 points
~ Vinny O'Hare ~

Green Tailed Jay Butterfly

Do ye not comprehend that we are worms born
to bring forth the angelic butterfly that flieth
unto judgment without screen?
~ *Dante Alighieri* ~

Heliconius Erato Butterfly

Butterflies are like Rainbows
The longer you stare at them
The prettier they get
~ Vinny O'Hare ~

Indian Leaf Butterfly – Closed

A caterpillar who seeks to know himself would
never become a butterfly
~ *Andre Gide* ~

Indian Leaf Butterfly – Open

An Indian Butterfly Legend
If anyone desires a wish to come true they must
capture a butterfly and whisper that wish to it.
Since they make no sound, they can't tell the
wish to anyone but the Great Spirit.
So by making the wish and releasing the
butterfly it will be taken to the
heavens and be granted.

Malachite Butterfly Hanging Upside Down

There is nothing better than
seeing a butterfly go from flower to flower to
take your problems out of mind.
~ *Vinny O'Hare* ~

Orange Tiger Butterfly – Closed

Orange Tiger Butterfly – Open

Paperkite (Rice Paper) Butterfly
One of the largest butterflies, and certainly one
of the most beautiful

Butterflies...flowers that fly and all but sing.
~ Robert Frost ~

Postman Butterfly

The butterfly counts not months but moments,
and has time enough.
~ *Rabindranath Tagore* ~

Sailor Butterfly

If nothing ever changed,
there would be no butterflies
~ *Anonymous* ~

Scarlet Mormon Butterfly

On the eighth day God created butterflies
to make the planet prettier
~ Vinny O'Hare ~

Shoemaker Butterfly

They seemed to come suddenly
upon happiness as if they had surprised a
butterfly in the winter woods
~ *Edith Wharton* ~

Zebra Longwing Butterfly

A Butterfly Lights Beside Us
A butterfly lights beside us, like a sunbeam...
and for a brief moment it's glory and
beauty belong to our world...
but then it flies on again, and although we wish
it could have stayed,
we are so thankful to have seen it at all.
~ Author Unknown ~

More fun butterfly stuff, including
butterfly art and prints:
http://CoolButterflies.com/

Follow us on Facebook to find out when
Flowers With Wings Volume 2 and
Butterflies A to Z are published and to see
cool butterflies all the time.
Facebook.com/CoolButterflies

All our butterfly photographs are taken of live
butterflies in the wild or in sanctioned butterfly
conservatories.

Other Books by Deborah Carney

http://loxly.com/go/dcauthor

If you enjoyed our book please go to the book page at Amazon and leave your comments, we really want to hear what you think!

NightFire Inspiration Series
http://loxly.com/go/inspire

Flowers With Wings Butterfly Series
http://loxly.com/go/bhwings

Poetry and Peonies Series
http://poetryandpeonies.com

The Southwest Gallery Series
http://thesouthwestgallery.com

Fun Funky Art Cats, Flowers, Cars, NYC, Animals
http://funfunkyart.com

Weirder Than Marshmallows Book of Essays by Dan Fogg
http://WeirderThanMarshmallows.com

Book Cover Design by www.Lesruba.com

Book Cover Photography by www.DeborahCarney.com

DEDICATION

My books are dedicated to my children and family:

Dan – who didn't let his disability stop him from achieving his dreams

Chris – showed us how to live even when it was hard.

Liz – more than a daughter to me, and more than a sister to her brothers.

To my Dad – Who bought me my first camera and told me I could do anything

To my Sister Kathleen – For the book we couldn't write together

To the love of my life that rescued me and

taught me how to love and how to follow my dreams.

In Memoriam
Daniel Fogg (1980 – 2002)
Christopher Fogg (1978 – 2006)

"People have ideas all the time, ambition is just the stubbornness to follow through."

Daniel Fogg, 2001

We are where we are supposed to be,
when we are supposed to be there.

~ Deborah Carney, 2012